# READING SYSTEM

## STUDENT WORKBOOK ONE B

**THIRD EDITION**

by Barbara A. Wilson

Wilson Language Training
175 West Main Street
Millbury, Massachusetts  01527-1441
(508) 865-5699

ISBN 1-56778-094-6          Student Workbook One B          Item# SW1B


The Wilson Reading System is published by:

Wilson Language Training Corp.
175 West Main Street
Millbury, MA 01527-1441

Tap out sounds. Read the word. Write the letter(s) for each sound in the boxes.

bath = ☐ ☐ ☐          con = ☐ ☐ ☐

mash = ☐ ☐ ☐          hub = ☐ ☐ ☐

lap = ☐ ☐ ☐           sash = ☐ ☐ ☐

fat = ☐ ☐ ☐           dim = ☐ ☐ ☐

chat = ☐ ☐ ☐          pod = ☐ ☐ ☐

cash = ☐ ☐ ☐          tax = ☐ ☐ ☐

jab = ☐ ☐ ☐           dock = ☐ ☐ ☐

cap = ☐ ☐ ☐           sag = ☐ ☐ ☐

hack = ☐ ☐ ☐          lab = ☐ ☐ ☐

pub = ☐ ☐ ☐           Sis = ☐ ☐ ☐

posh = ☐ ☐ ☐          pin = ☐ ☐ ☐

yen = ☐ ☐ ☐           pun = ☐ ☐ ☐

chug = ☐ ☐ ☐          quip = ☐ ☐ ☐

vat = ☐ ☐ ☐           hack = ☐ ☐ ☐

dab = ☐ ☐ ☐           fib = ☐ ☐ ☐

**Tap out sounds, blend into a word and write the word on the line.**

| r | o | b | = _____ |

| n | o | d | = _____ |

| m | o | p | = _____ |

| r | o | t | = _____ |

| g | a | p | = _____ |

| r | i | m | = _____ |

| l | o | g | = _____ |

| p | a | l | = _____ |

| d | o | t | = _____ |

| h | i | p | = _____ |

| r | i | ch | = _____ |

| m | a | p | = _____ |

| l | i | d | = _____ |

| b | e | d | = _____ |

| r | a | sh | = _____ |


| qu | i | z | = _____ |

| ch | u | m | = _____ |

| n | i | ck | = _____ |

| s | o | d | = _____ |

| p | e | ck | = _____ |

| r | a | ck | = _____ |

| j | a | ck | = _____ |

| c | o | d | = _____ |

| p | o | d | = _____ |

| h | a | sh | = _____ |

| b | i | d | = _____ |

| l | a | d | = _____ |

| l | u | sh | = _____ |

| b | i | n | = _____ |

| s | u | m | = _____ |

Choose a vowel to make a real word.  Write the word on the line.  Read the words.

| a | o |
|---|---|
| m __ p _____ | |
| l __ b _____ | |
| l __ g _____ | |

| a | i |
|---|---|
| ch __ p _____ | |
| b __ g _____ | |
| p __ th _____ | |

| e | i |
|---|---|
| r __ d _____ | |
| j __ g _____ | |
| b __ g _____ | |

| o | u |
|---|---|
| j __ b _____ | |
| h __ t _____ | |
| m __ p _____ | |

| a | u |
|---|---|
| t __ g _____ | |
| r __ p _____ | |
| g __ g _____ | |

| e | i |
|---|---|
| r __ g _____ | |
| th __ m _____ | |
| r __ b _____ | |

| o | u |
|---|---|
| m __ th _____ | |
| l __ ck _____ | |
| th __ d _____ | |

| a | i |
|---|---|
| sh __ p _____ | |
| l __ ck _____ | |
| f __ sh _____ | |

**Tap out the sounds, blend into a word and write the word on the line.**

| n | u | t | = _____ | | m | a | th | = _____ |

| b | u | g | = _____ | | m | e | sh | = _____ |

| h | u | b | = _____ | | r | i | g | = _____ |

| p | u | p | = _____ | | sh | o | d | = _____ |

| r | u | n | = _____ | | th | u | g | = _____ |

| b | u | t | = _____ | | r | i | m | = _____ |

| m | u | g | = _____ | | j | u | t | = _____ |

| r | u | t | = _____ | | sh | u | n | = _____ |

| ch | i | n | = _____ | | t | u | x | = _____ |

| ch | o | p | = _____ | | ch | a | t | = _____ |

| ch | a | t | = _____ | | l | a | x | = _____ |

| p | a | th | = _____ | | g | u | t | = _____ |

| ch | u | m | = _____ | | k | i | n | = _____ |

| r | i | ch | = _____ | | l | a | sh | = _____ |

| th | u | g | = _____ | | ch | a | p | = _____ |

Read the sentence. Select the correct word from the box.
Write the word on the line. Reread the completed sentence.

1. This job *is* not so much _____ .

   | fun |
   | fin |

2. *The* tot got *a* hug *from his* _____ .

   | mom |
   | mop |

3. Tom got in *the* hot _____ .

   | tug |
   | tub |

4. *The* cub *is* on *the* _____ .

   | pat |
   | path |

5. *The* chap got *the* pig in *the* _____ .

   | big |
   | bag |

6. Jim had *to* chop *the* _____ .

   | log |
   | lot |

7. *The* moth *is* in *the* _____ .

   | cop |
   | cup |

8. Tim had *a* nap on *the* _____ .

   | cot |
   | cat |

9. *The* gal hit *her* chin on *the* _____ .

   | jot |
   | jug |

10. Pat *will* jog on *the* _____ .

   | path |
   | pug |

Write the vowels in the box on the blank spaces to form words.  Read the words.  Rewrite the whole
word on the lines provided.

1.  | a, i |  f_t        f_t

    _____     _____

2.  | a, e, i |  s_t      s_t      s_t

    _____     _____     _____

3.  | i, o |  sh_p      sh_p

    _____     _____

4.  | a, e, i |  b_d      b_d      b_d

    _____     _____     _____

5.  | i, o, u |  d_g      d_g      d_g

    _____     _____     _____

6.  | a, e, i, o |  p_t      p_t      p_t      p_t

    _____     _____     _____     _____

7.  | a, i |  d_sh      d_sh

    _____     _____

8.  | e, i, u |  h_m      h_m      h_m

    _____     _____     _____

9.  | e, o, u |  n_t      n_t      n_t

    _____     _____     _____

10. | a, i, o |  ch_p      ch_p      ch_p

    _____     _____     _____

**Draw a line to connect the words that rhyme in each box. Read the words.**

| | |
|---|---|
| bash | chap |
| tap | dash |
| yum | gum |

| | |
|---|---|
| mix | fix |
| zip | dish |
| fish | lip |

| | |
|---|---|
| wax | quiz |
| quip | tax |
| whiz | tip |

| | |
|---|---|
| vim | bet |
| rig | whim |
| yet | big |

| | |
|---|---|
| shag | cot |
| kin | wag |
| shot | win |

| | |
|---|---|
| yen | fish |
| wish | pen |
| chop | shop |

| | |
|---|---|
| deck | neck |
| dud | dab |
| nab | mud |

| | |
|---|---|
| sack | nod |
| hem | lack |
| sod | them |

**Select one word from each match to write on the lines below.**

_____ _____ _____ _____

_____ _____ _____ _____

_____ _____ _____ _____

_____ _____ _____ _____

_____ _____ _____ _____

**Tap out sounds. Read the word. Write the letter(s) for each sound in the box.**

back = ☐ ☐ ☐          hog = ☐ ☐ ☐

map = ☐ ☐ ☐          mix = ☐ ☐ ☐

bib = ☐ ☐ ☐          dish = ☐ ☐ ☐

hit = ☐ ☐ ☐          whiz = ☐ ☐ ☐

chat = ☐ ☐ ☐          rich = ☐ ☐ ☐

cab = ☐ ☐ ☐          sap = ☐ ☐ ☐

hip = ☐ ☐ ☐          bath = ☐ ☐ ☐

cap = ☐ ☐ ☐          dab = ☐ ☐ ☐

chip = ☐ ☐ ☐          hush = ☐ ☐ ☐

pot = ☐ ☐ ☐          chin = ☐ ☐ ☐

bath = ☐ ☐ ☐          quit = ☐ ☐ ☐

cub = ☐ ☐ ☐          shock = ☐ ☐ ☐

chap = ☐ ☐ ☐          lob = ☐ ☐ ☐

gum = ☐ ☐ ☐          whim = ☐ ☐ ☐

much = ☐ ☐ ☐          with = ☐ ☐ ☐

**Tap out sounds, blend into a nonsense word and write the word on the line.**     !@#$%

| w | o | b | = _____ | | v | a | sh | = _____ |
| l | a | t | = _____ | | d | a | x | = _____ |
| f | e | p | = _____ | | r | a | b | = _____ |
| t | e | z | = _____ | | qu | o | p | = _____ |
| b | i | x | = _____ | | f | a | sh | = _____ |
| j | u | p | = _____ | | ch | e | z | = _____ |
| k | i | z | = _____ | | r | e | m | = _____ |
| l | o | m | = _____ | | z | e | g | = _____ |
| qu | i | m | = _____ | | s | o | t | = _____ |
| f | e | g | = _____ | | b | i | sh | = _____ |
| s | i | th | = _____ | | w | o | g | = _____ |
| p | o | th | = _____ | | m | e | d | = _____ |
| b | e | p | = _____ | | j | i | t | = _____ |
| g | o | m | = _____ | | h | o | sh | = _____ |
| t | e | m | = _____ | | d | i | th | = _____ |

**Select letters to write on the lines before and after each vowel to make real words. Read the words.**

| b | p | t | th |
|---|---|---|---|
| __ a __ | | | |
| __ a __ | | | |
| __ a __ | | | |
| __ a __ | | | |

| d | p | sh | l |
|---|---|---|---|
| __ i __ | | | |
| __ i __ | | | |
| __ i __ | | | |
| __ i __ | | | |

| b | d | g | t |
|---|---|---|---|
| __ e __ | | | |
| __ e __ | | | |
| __ e __ | | | |
| __ e __ | | | |

| sh | t | p | g |
|---|---|---|---|
| __ o __ | | | |
| __ o __ | | | |
| __ o __ | | | |
| __ o __ | | | |

| ch | g | b | t |
|---|---|---|---|
| __ u __ | | | |
| __ u __ | | | |
| __ u __ | | | |
| __ u __ | | | |

| b | f | g | x |
|---|---|---|---|
| __ o __ | | | |
| __ o __ | | | |
| __ o __ | | | |
| __ o __ | | | |

| l | p | t | ck |
|---|---|---|---|
| __ a __ | | | |
| __ a __ | | | |
| __ a __ | | | |
| __ a __ | | | |

| s | ck | t | p |
|---|---|---|---|
| __ i __ | | | |
| __ i __ | | | |
| __ i __ | | | |
| __ i __ | | | |

| fix | zat | quim |
|-----|-----|------|
| web | chug | wid |
| lig | quit | chip |
| yut | lack | moth |
| sash | zad | thud |
| chum | niz | hut |
| lag | quat | hup |
| fap | shot | bud |
| rap | rich | hib |
| rop | bin | hog |

**Write the real words on the lines below.**

| _____ | _____ | _____ |
|-----|-----|------|
| _____ | _____ | _____ |
| _____ | _____ | _____ |
| _____ | _____ | _____ |
| _____ | _____ | _____ |

**Read the sentence. Select the best word to complete each sentence from the box. Use each word only once. Write the word on the line. Reread the completed sentence.**

| dish | lip | job | shed | path |
|------|-----|-----|------|------|
| met | bus | had | moth | wig |

1.  Tim hid *the* cat in *the* _____.

2.  *The* fish in that _____ *will* rot.

3.  Yes, Meg had *to* jog on that _____.

4.  Tim _____ *a* nap.

5.  Bob got *a* cut on *his* _____.

6.  Beth had *a* _____.

7.  Ted _____ Ben at *the* shop.

8.  *A* big _____ *is* in *the* pot.

9.  Did Tom get *the* _____?

10. Tim *will* hop on that _____.

Read each word and segment the sounds.  Write the word under the correct vowel by placing one sound on each line.

| pod | gal | thin | web | quit | shed | sash |
| peck | mob | ship | shop | cub | such | duck |
| pad | wick | hush | mesh | shag | lob | rut |

**a**

\_\_\_  \_\_\_  \_\_\_

\_\_\_  \_\_\_  \_\_\_

\_\_\_  \_\_\_  \_\_\_

\_\_\_  \_\_\_  \_\_\_

**e**

\_\_\_  \_\_\_  \_\_\_

\_\_\_  \_\_\_  \_\_\_

\_\_\_  \_\_\_  \_\_\_

\_\_\_  \_\_\_  \_\_\_

**i**

\_\_\_  \_\_\_  \_\_\_

\_\_\_  \_\_\_  \_\_\_

\_\_\_  \_\_\_  \_\_\_

\_\_\_  \_\_\_  \_\_\_

**o**

\_\_\_  \_\_\_  \_\_\_

\_\_\_  \_\_\_  \_\_\_

\_\_\_  \_\_\_  \_\_\_

\_\_\_  \_\_\_  \_\_\_

**u**

\_\_\_  \_\_\_  \_\_\_

\_\_\_  \_\_\_  \_\_\_

\_\_\_  \_\_\_  \_\_\_

\_\_\_  \_\_\_  \_\_\_

\_\_\_  \_\_\_  \_\_\_

**Sound out these real and nonsense words.  Circle the real words.**

| cob | gap | mob |
| tug | hush | hush |
| shed | jud | lack |
| quim | fib | quop |
| sag | dash | gal |
| rash | quit | moth |
| whiz | dob | lish |
| lat | shock | pal |
| dock | huz | chat |
| dax | lid | chob |

**Write the real words on the lines below.**

_____     _____     _____

_____     _____     _____

_____     _____     _____

_____     _____     _____

_____     _____     _____

_____     _____     _____

## <u>The Jog</u>

_____ *A* big log *was* on *the* path.

_____ It *was* not hot *and* Jim did *a* lap.

_____ *The* run *was* not much fun.

_____ Jim got up *to* jog on *the* path.

_____ Jim fell in *a* rut *and* hit *his* chin.

**Rewrite the sentences above in the correct order on the lines below.**

1. _____

2. _____

3. _____

4. _____

5. _____

Select bonus letters at the top of the box to make real words.  If more than one selection
makes a word, choose one.  Read the words.

| ff | ll | ss |
|---|---|---|
| we _____ | | |
| o _____ | | |
| hu _____ | | |

| ff | ll | ss |
|---|---|---|
| whi _____ | | |
| mi _____ | | |
| cu _____ | | |

| ff | ll | ss |
|---|---|---|
| wi _____ | | |
| me _____ | | |
| be _____ | | |

| ff | ll | ss |
|---|---|---|
| lu _____ | | |
| qui _____ | | |
| ti _____ | | |

| ff | ll | ss |
|---|---|---|
| mi _____ | | |
| fe _____ | | |
| chi _____ | | |

| ff | ll | ss |
|---|---|---|
| du _____ | | |
| ma _____ | | |
| ki _____ | | |

| ff | ll | ss |
|---|---|---|
| hi _____ | | |
| si _____ | | |
| jo _____ | | |

| ff | ll | ss |
|---|---|---|
| bi _____ | | |
| mo _____ | | |
| mu _____ | | |

**Sound out these real words. Add bonus letters to words that need them.**

| | | |
|---|---|---|
| dul | wish | cuf |
| led | shel | rub |
| shut | mos | keg |
| fus | dil | pit |
| mis | sad | wil |
| moth | kis | mil |
| bath | puf | dig |
| tif | lid | ches |
| bil | hip | shag |
| gag | yap | pil |

**Write words with bonus letters on the lines below.**

| | | |
|---|---|---|
| _____ | _____ | _____ |
| _____ | _____ | _____ |
| _____ | _____ | _____ |
| _____ | _____ | _____ |
| _____ | _____ | _____ |

**Read the sentence. Select the word with the correct spelling from the box and write it on the line.**

1. ken had *to* get *the* _____

bel
bell

2. *i* wish that *i* had *a* _____

dog
dogg

3. will Beth miss _____

Rus
Russ

4. mom *was* mad *and* in *a* _____

huf
huff

5. ben met jill at *his* _____

job
jobb

**Copy the sentences above on the lines below. Add capital letters and punctuation.**

1. _____

2. _____

3. _____

4. _____

5. _____

**Read each sentence. Add bonus letters to the words that need them.**

1. *I* bet Nell wil   pas   in math.

2. Bev got *a* chil   in *the* tub.

3. Jim wil   mis   Liz.

4. Beth wil   fil   *the* pot on *the* sil
   with sod.

5. *The* bos   got *a* bel   *for the* shop.

_____

**Rewrite each sentence correctly on the lines below.**

1._____

2._____

3._____

4._____

5._____

**Sound out these real words. Add bonus letters to words that need them.**
**Circle the words that contain the <u>all</u> sound.**

| | | |
|---|---|---|
| dil | mal | lob |
| nip | huf | fal |
| that | mad | buf |
| hal | sat | lid |
| gap | wal | mis |
| bas | yap | ches |
| had | shut | cal |
| bag | tif | cob |
| rap | tal | rip |
| cuf | his | bal |
| sub | quil | thug |
| yam | mif | dul |
| mes | dock | shap |
| whip | mob | bel |
| kit | muff | hug |

Read the sentence. Select the correct word from the box to complete the sentence.
Write the word on the line. Reread the completed sentence. Use each word in the box only once.

| | | | | |
|---|---|---|---|---|
| mall | fall | wall | tall | call |
| all | ball | hall | doll | gall |

1. Ben *and* Beth will *go to the* _____ to shop.

2. Ted will _____ Liz at six *p.m.*

3. Did Ed get *the* _____ in *the* net?

4. _____ *the* kids will jog on that path.

5. Jim *is* not _____ , but he can get *the* ball
   on *the* rim!

6. *Do* not run in *the* _____ .

7. Did Tom _____ on that mat?

8. Dad had to fix the _____ so that the fox
   can not get in the hen pen.

9. *The* tot had *a* _____ on *her* lap.

10. That man had *a* lot *of* _____ .

**Tap out sounds, blend into a word, cover the letters and write the word on the line.**

| t | an | = _____ | p | a | ss | = _____ |

| t | i | ff | = _____ | k | i | ll | = _____ |

| ch | i | ll | = _____ | ch | um | = _____ |

| f | an | = _____ | sh | e | ll | = _____ |

| b | all | = _____ | ch | e | ss | = _____ |

| sh | am | = _____ | y | am | = _____ |

| h | u | ff | = _____ | m | o | ss | = _____ |

| r | am | = _____ | c | an | = _____ |

| b | an | = _____ | f | u | ss | = _____ |

| l | a | ss | = _____ | th | an | = _____ |

| b | am | = _____ | t | e | ll | = _____ |

| d | u | ll | = _____ | P | am | = _____ |

| m | e | ss | = _____ | b | i | ll | = _____ |

| m | an | = _____ | j | am | = _____ |

| h | am | = _____ | j | o | ss | = _____ |

Read the words. Find and circle all <u>am</u> and <u>an</u> letter combinations. Cover the word and write it on the line. Uncover the word and check the spelling.

| fish _____ | zip _____ | chap _____ |
| can _____ | sob _____ | ban _____ |
| Dan _____ | web _____ | shot _____ |
| chum _____ | pan _____ | vim _____ |
| wham _____ | yak _____ | am _____ |
| rod _____ | ham _____ | quill _____ |
| chess _____ | fun _____ | fan _____ |
| man _____ | Jan _____ | bid _____ |
| dash _____ | ran _____ | Sam _____ |
| Pam _____ | lag _____ | moth _____ |
| fog _____ | sun _____ | bash _____ |
| gull _____ | shun _____ | dam _____ |
| run _____ | yam _____ | jot _____ |
| bet _____ | Chad _____ | sap _____ |
| sham _____ | pad _____ | jut _____ |

**Read the sentences. Find and circle or highlight the _am_ or _an_ letter combinations.**

1. Pam can not get *the* gum off *the* map.

2. Did Dan pass *the* math quiz?

3. Sam had *the* fish in *the* pan.

4. Beth will get jam at *the* shop.

5. *The* man will fuss *about the* loss.

6. Jan had *the* cash *to* get *the* bat
   *and* ball.

7. Did Ben sell *the* tan van yet?

8. Rich did not get *the* ham.

9. *I* am sad, but *I* will be *O.K.*

10. Gus ran *to* get *the* fan in *the* shed.

---

**Write the _am_ and _an_ words on the lines below.**

**am**             **an**

_____   _____  |  _____   _____

_____   _____  |  _____   _____

_____           |  _____   _____

                            |  _____   _____

**Select letters from each box to make real words. Read the words.**

| z | p | ch | r | d |
|---|---|----|---|---|
| ___ am | | | | |
| ___ am | | | | |
| ___ am | | | | |

| th | h | s | y | f |
|----|---|---|---|---|
| ___ am | | | | |
| ___ am | | | | |
| ___ am | | | | |

| qu | j | b | g | wh |
|----|---|---|---|----|
| ___ am | | | | |
| ___ am | | | | |
| ___ am | | | | |

| f | ch | v | y | r |
|---|----|---|---|---|
| ___ an | | | | |
| ___ an | | | | |
| ___ an | | | | |

| m | t | qu | g | c |
|---|---|----|---|---|
| ___ an | | | | |
| ___ an | | | | |
| ___ an | | | | |

| sh | d | b | p | z |
|----|---|---|---|---|
| ___ an | | | | |
| ___ an | | | | |
| ___ an | | | | |

**Write the words above on the lines below.**

_____          _____

_____          _____

_____          _____

_____          _____

_____          _____

_____          _____

_____          _____

Underline the baseword and circle the s . Write the baseword on the line. Read the entire word.

ribs _____          tubs _____          pads _____

rugs _____          wigs _____          pals _____

moths_____          bags _____          shops_____

ships _____          bells _____          hugs _____

caps _____          chips _____          fans _____

fins _____          sheds _____          kits _____

dogs _____          pills _____          nuts _____

shells_____          cats _____          subs _____

guns _____          kids _____          lips _____

balls _____          jobs _____          logs _____

puns _____          yams _____          pecks_____

robs _____          mobs _____          bins _____

lads _____          yells _____          whips_____

docks _____          nags _____          racks _____

quills _____          lacks _____          rigs _____

Read the words. Write s̲ on the line if the s̲ has the /s/ sound and z̲ if it has the /z/ sound.

| | | | |
|---|---|---|---|
| chips | /__/ | pals | /__/ |
| pills | /__/ | cops | /__/ |
| dots | /__/ | bells | /__/ |
| guns | /__/ | pets | /__/ |
| lips | /__/ | kids | /__/ |
| subs | /__/ | puns | /__/ |
| chums | /__/ | bins | /__/ |
| thugs | /__/ | peds | /__/ |
| pecks | /__/ | yells | /__/ |
| quills | /__/ | racks | /__/ |
| sums | /__/ | rigs | /__/ |
| whips | /__/ | tics | /__/ |
| jabs | /__/ | rots | /__/ |
| dubs | /__/ | hags | /__/ |
| lacks | /__/ | kits | /__/ |

**Read the sentence. Select the correct word from the box to complete the sentence. Write the word on the line. Reread the completed sentence. Use each word in the box only once.**

| cats | rugs | malls | cots | jobs |
|------|------|-------|------|------|

1. Mom had *the* kids on _____ *for a* nap.

2. Yes, *the* _____ *and* dogs *are* pals!

3. Mobs will shop at *the* _____ .

4. *The* dog sheds on *the* _____ .

5. Sid quits _____ *so* that *he* can jog on *a* whim.

**Write the baseword and circle the suffix in each sentence above. Write the basewords on the lines below.**

1._____  _____

2._____  _____  _____

3._____  _____

4._____  _____

5._____  _____

**Read the real and nonsense words. Add _s_ and read the word. Circle all the real words. Cross out the nonsense words. Write the real words on the lines at the bottom of the page.**

cap__          bap__          juff__

bip__          rot__          sep__

fom__          sum__          fam__

whip__         jeg__          chill__

zup__          chim__         jab__

pack__         quall__        shob__

gam__          mob__          fib__

yell__         rack__         thig__

win__          gog__          dip__

rab__          deck__         shut__

_____  _____  _____

_____  _____  _____

_____  _____  _____

_____  _____  _____

_____  _____  _____